KATHRYN M.IRELAND
INSPIRED BY…

KATHRYN M. IRELAND
INSPIRED BY . . .

GIBBS SMITH
TO ENRICH AND INSPIRE HUMANKIND

To Gitana and Greta

—RIP—

The best Jack Russells ever!

CONTENTS

FOREWORD

{ by Lady Annabel Goldsmith }

I first met Kathryn when she was a little girl, attending the same school as my daughter India Jane and my nieces. She swiftly became part of the tribe of children who would play in the large garden of my enchanting little Regency house, Pelham Cottage, where the garden door was never shut and everyone wandered in whenever they were passing. She remained in my life from then on until she moved to Los Angeles, but we stayed in constant touch. And then one day she appeared at my new home in Richmond—Ormeley Lodge—with a very tall, charming, and rather hirsute husband, even more energetic than herself, named Gary. She then proceeded to have three boys, one of whom is my godson.

Kathryn's energy and talent for any artistic project was obvious from early on, but she told me she was first inspired by Pelham Cottage—which had been exquisitely decorated and refurbished by my husband Mark Birley, who had already established his famous nightclub Annabel's, which he named after me—and later by my second home, Ormeley Lodge, where Kathryn frequently stayed when she came over from America.

Despite having three babies, Kathryn proceeded to decorate many houses in LA. By then she was producing the most exquisite fabrics and also had an office in London. A lot of her fabrics have been used at Ormeley and have been greatly admired.

But Kathryn is more than just a bundle of talent; she is one of the kindest and most generous people I have ever met, with a sense of humor exactly on a par with mine. We cannot get through a telephone conversation or just be together without collapsing with laughter. We also share a love of houses and interiors, although regrettably, I do not share her talent.

INTRODUCTION

This book is not about me; it's about the friends and colleagues whose individuality and passion for design have inspired my life and my work over the years. My purpose with *Inspired By* is to take you on a personalized journey through an array of homes that reflect the diversity and eclecticism of people in my life. Some are homes of the interior design elite; others are houses designed by friends with careers far removed from the sphere of the applied arts; but all of these friends share three attributes: they're innately creative; they have the confidence to be original; and their homes collectively express the ambient consequence of living passionately and stylishly.

Just as every friend has a story to tell, so does every house. Because a house is not just a portrait of the people who live there; it is also a biography. The most dynamic interiors are those that best reflect their owners' passions, memories, hobbies, talents, and skills. The "stories" in this book abide by that precept, and the results are unique atmospheres that mix the rare, the antique, and the unexpected with the everyday yet always feel fresh, effortless, and livable. All of my friends understand that to surround themselves with objects they love creates instant comfort and coherence. And, in the end, this is really the method that makes a house magic—creating

deeply personal interiors by building them up over the years with love and true passion *in layers.*

From a young age, I knew my true calling was houses. And not just stately manors or grand estates. (In France I now spend most of my time in a converted cow barn.) For me, going on play dates meant I got to visit my friends' houses and experience them. I loved exploring the rooms and the feeling that came over me if the house was well-lived-in. My mother was a genius at creating a home and entertaining guests. She did it with such ease. From our flat in London to our cottage in Scotland, my friends were always welcome, two to a bed and as many as could squeeze around the table. Ours was the house everyone wanted to come to because my mother knew how to embrace mistakes, imperfection, and the chaos of real life. It's a tribute to my mother that she made all of my friends feel so welcome, so appreciated, and so at ease.

I feel that way about all of the houses in this book, whether at Michael's, where I stopped for a glass of champagne one night, or at Annabel's, where I lived for over a year; weeks with Carina in Devon, afternoons and evenings at Windsor's, Baby's, and Martyn's. I hope all of the homes included here will provide you with an array of inspiring ideas, and I hope none of my friends ever stop creating.

EUGENIA MARCOU

{ The Collector }

Gina is my incredibly stylish, cultured, globe-trotting Greek friend who has called London home her entire life. We all know how much real work goes into composing spectacular environments; the trick is making it look easy and effortless. And this is perhaps Gina's greatest strength. Whether she's browsing 1stdibs or eBay, or trekking around Alfie's Market in North London, she has a talent for discovering exquisite pieces. I don't know anyone with better "sourcing" karma than Gina. It helps that she has an eye for excellence and an innate drift towards anything chic, whether old, new, or recycled. She is also a meticulous overseer with complete command of her vision.

At her residence in Notting Hill, a beautiful six-story house in one of the most coveted neighborhoods in London, she served as architect, interior designer, and project manager. The house opens onto beautiful communal gardens. Though the trendiest, most *au courant* shops and restaurants in London are a mere stone's throw away, when you gaze out the back of Gina's house toward the gardens, you can easily imagine being in the pastoral English countryside.

Being with Gina is like being with me! She's brilliant at preplanning, organizing, anticipating logistical problems and beating them to the punch. A few years ago, my son Oscar and I were her guests for ten delightful days in Cuba. Every side trip, every meal, every minute was meticulously prearranged—the fun was effortless. And when I'm in London, popping back and forth between Gina's house and Gaby's, it's the most homesick I ever feel for my hometown.

WHAT KINDS OF ANTIQUES DO YOU LIKE? Furniture from all centuries, from the most ornate to the most minimal. In the house, there is French and English, 18th-century to 20th-century; Poul Kjærholm, Carlo Mollino, '70s Pieff chairs, etc.

WHAT ADVICE WOULD YOU GIVE TO PEOPLE BUYING THEIR FIRST HOUSE? Don't look at decorating magazines.

WHAT THREE THINGS COULD YOU NOT LIVE WITHOUT? The sea, the past, and good shoes.

YOUR FAVORITE FILM? *Some Like It Hot.*

WHERE DO YOU CALL HOME? The Mediterranean blue.

IF YOU COULD LIVE IN ANY ERA, WHICH WOULD IT BE? Aesthetically, it would have to be the 1930s.

IF YOU COULD HAVE ANY PAINTINGS, WHAT WOULD YOU CHOOSE? Picasso's *La Baignade,* in the Peggy Guggenheim in Venice; it holds all paintings old and new within it. And Bronzino's *Portrait of Giovanni de' Medici*.

WHAT'S YOUR FAVORITE DISH? Fried artichokes.

YOUR CHILDHOOD OBSESSIONS? Archaeology, old stones, and underwater treasure.

WHAT DO YOU COLLECT? Well I've never found the perfect sofa, so the search goes on.

HOW OFTEN DOES YOUR HOME CHANGE? Don't ask.

DO YOU PREFER SUNRISES OR SUNSETS? Best to see both and have a very long siesta in between.

would be so amazed if there were a next life, I would have to come back to this one and pack.

INSPIRED BY . . .

» Paint color of living room walls

» Red stripe of fabric on leading edges of the curtains

» Juxtaposition of modern and antiques

» Picasso next to Freud

» Bedroom opening onto the bathroom (pocket doors)

» Window treatments when necessary

» Minimal decorating

» Unique light fixtures

I admire Picasso's work. *You can't get away from him* and you don't want to.

JAMIE GOULD

{ The Weaver }

A few years after I had established myself as a designer of hand-printed textiles, I met Jamie Gould, an owner of Rogers and Goffigon, the renowned manufacturer of luxury, all-natural textiles. From that moment on, I relentlessly quizzed him on his craft, but he was always very gracious, very patient, and an endless source of knowledge regarding everything from technique to which mills were best to work with.

Jamie is one of those people whose generosity is boundless. He is very long-suffering, and his love for his Corgis is endearing. We share a love for France and anything English. He is easily teased, and in all the years and time I've spent with him he has only once gotten really irritated with me. Understandably. We were in St. Barts and he asked me to get some money out of the cash machine to tip the staff at the end our stay. I managed to punch in the wrong code number too many times and the machine ate the card. *Zut alors!*

I am lucky enough to call Jamie one of my closest friends. He and his photographer wife, Dale, live in an 18th-century farmhouse in pastoral Greenwich, Connecticut. The house is idyllically situated among rolling green hills, chicken coops, and faded red barns. Jamie converted his own barn into a bespoke weaving mill, where he designs and produces hand-loomed carpets.

A few years ago, the Goulds added a formal living room, dining room, and master suite to the original structure of small, cozy rooms that connect well to the new wing. These beautifully produced rooms, filled with Gustavian antiques, hand-painted wallpapers, Dale's photographs, and Jamie's cloth are all testament to the talent that resides there.

"No other artifact *visually marks the passage of historic time,* of stability and change, of cultural continuity and flux more than does architecture." —BERNARD HERMAN

WHAT INSPIRES YOU?

FAVORITE MOVIE? *The Lives of Others, by* von Donnersmarck.

ARTIST? Vermeer.

COUNTRY? UK, especially England and Scotland.

ARCHITECT/DESIGNER? John Pawson for interior design; Robert Adams.

CITIES? London and Los Angeles.

CULTURE? 18th-century British, all Italian.

AUTHORS? Stendhal and Balzac.

BOOK? *Don Quixote.*

SINGERS? Aretha and Ella.

DRINKS? Tequila and Single Malt.

WHAT BEACHES DO YOU LIKE? Ones in the Caribbean with no hotels on them.

IF YOU COULD CHOOSE ANY PAINTING FOR YOUR ENTRY, WHAT WOULD IT BE? George Stubbs' *Zebra.*

INSPIRED BY . . .

» Muted paint colors

» Kitchen cabinets limited to a minimum

» Diverse ages/patinas of the furniture

» Hallway-cum-library

» Vintage textiles

» Colors, furnishings, and fabrics all in sync

» Timeless use of wallpapers

BARRY DIXON

{ Gentleman Farmer }

Arriving at Elway Hall, Barry Dixon's magnificent estate in Virginia, one always feels transported to another time and place. But arriving at nighttime, as I first did, is inexpressibly dramatic. Childhood memories of visiting friends for the weekend with my parents and arriving late on Friday evenings in total darkness, unable to discern the landscape or the architecture, came flooding back. The only difference between Elway and its English counterparts is that Barry's home is gloriously lit up, so that the grandeur of the house, if not the rolling countryside, is immediately legible. In the morning, I felt as if I was awaking to a dream.

With his movie-star good looks, Southern charm, and extraordinary eye for detail, Barry is as unique and unforgettable as his home. He is that rare breed of decorator that has elevated interior design to a high art form.

I've stayed at Elway many times, and whenever I return I see things that escaped my eye on previous visits. His ability to layer is what inspires me the most about him, not to mention his amazing singing voice and dance moves! Barry is a great host and looks after all his guests with equal affection, attention, and generosity.

His collections are immense, from antique china to out-of-print books. The level of detail in his home is beyond description, right down to the flowers he handpicks from his own cutting garden and places beside each guest's bed.

MY FAVORITE ROOM

in the house is

the library.

but big changes SELDOM.

WHAT INSPIRES YOU?

MOVIES? Hitchcock's *Rebecca,* with its wildly grandiose, moody fantasy of a home; *Manderlay;* and *Auntie Mame,* with the topsy-turvy, madly creative makeovers of Mame's NYC apartment.

ART? Oh, where to start—or stop? The works of Rothko, Titian, Twombly, Nevelson, Vermeer.

COUNTRIES? Italy and the African continent.

ARCHITECTS/INTERIOR DESIGNERS? Sir Edwin Lutyens, Richard Neutra, Sir John Soane, Renzo Mongiardino, David Hicks, Elsie de Wolfe, and Albert Hadley.

ANIMAL? Elephants! Also birds and anything with horns.

CITY? Istanbul, or should I say Constantinople, the gateway between East and West.

ANTIQUE? I adore Anglo-Raj pieces from the late-19th/early 20th century—again, that mix!

FLOWERS? Tuberoses for their ethereal scent, large dinner-plate dahlias for their color and look, peonies for both.

AUTHORS? Daphne du Maurier, Eudora Welty, Flannery O'Conner, John Steinbeck, Harper Lee.

YOUR FAVORITE SINGERS? Contemporary, Adele. Timeless, Sinatra, Fitzgerald, et. al.

PLACE YOU'VE DISCOVERED OFF THE BEATEN PATH? Mombo Camp in Botswana's Okavango Delta—an inspiring place to go, again and again.

A FAVORITE QUOTE? "Grant me the serenity to accept the things I cannot change, the courage to change the things I can, and the wisdom to know the difference."

WHAT ADVICE DO YOU HAVE FOR PEOPLE BUYING THEIR FIRST HOUSE? Buy from the heart.

OTHER ADVICE? Everyone should have animals in their lives to be balanced.

IF YOU WEREN'T A DESIGNER, WHAT WOULD YOU DO? I think I'd teach. Or I'd like to be a curator in a museum.

DESCRIBE YOUR TYPICAL DAY? Up before dawn, drawing, coffee, and dog. Work with office/clients, lots of flying, literally and figuratively. Late dinner, time with Will, time for me, late to bed. Repeat. Average sleep, two to three hours per night.

WHAT ADJECTIVES DESCRIBE YOU? Interested, energetic, curious.

IF YOU WERE A COLOR, WHAT WOULD YOU BE? Verdant green.

IF YOU COULD LIVE IN ANY ERA, WHICH WOULD IT BE? The Edwardian period, early 20th century.

WHAT ARE YOUR BIGGEST PET PEEVES? Impolite people, car horns, warm diluted drinks.

WHAT ARE THE MOST IMPORTANT ELEMENTS OF A HOUSE? Hospitality, scale, and a sweet dog. And a crackling fire is a must!

My home is layered with things I love—pieces, people, and memories.

IN YOUR NEXT LIFE, WHO WOULD YOU LIKE TO BE? Truthfully, I'd be happy to be me all over again, to be a designer, surrounded by all the same people, the same loves. I think I could do it all better the second time around.

WHAT'S YOUR FAVORITE DISH? Pan-fried chicken with homemade yeast rolls, hot and buttered—childhood memories of my wonderful Southern grandmother.

YOUR CHILDHOOD OBSESSION? Drawing—in the margins of my school notebooks, on large tablets supplied by my parents, on magazine images, on any scrap of paper.

WHAT'S YOUR GUILTY PLEASURE? Old movie marathons, with others or alone. Only black-and-white will do, and screwball comedies are the best!

WHAT DO YOU COLLECT? China (creamware, basalt, and transferware) and books, books, books!

WHAT'S THE BEST PIECE OF ADVICE YOU HAVE EVER RECEIVED? "Do what you love to do in life, and 'work' won't be work." This is the only way to excel in your chosen field (from my father, by the way).

WHAT IS THE MOST COMMON MISTAKE PEOPLE MAKE? Doing what they think others expect them to do.

INSPIRED BY . . .

» Layering, layering, and more layering

» Every object relates to its setting

» Kitchen table inspired by a Lutyens design at Castle Drogo, Devon

» Entire walls of books

» Each room tells a story and is unique

» Bold use of one fabric throughout a room

» Use of curtains as wall-dividers

» Placing a bed in the center of the room, à la David Hicks

» Cutout "window" in bed headboard to let in light

» Bespoke William Morris wallpaper in modernized, custom colors

I could not live without
LOVE, LAUGHTER, AND HOPE,
esoterically speaking. Otherwise, hot water,
good French soap, and antiques.

MICHAEL BRUNO

{ The Entrepreneur }

Meeting Michael for the first time is almost a transformative experience. His magnetic personality would be at home in any century. I can picture him in a toga delivering infamous speeches in the Roman senate as easily as he shakes up convention in this century. Michael's boyish good looks, his diabolical charm, his spirit of adventure, and his compulsive creativity are his most reliable accomplices.

We crossed each other's paths some years ago and it was love at first sight. His online business, 1stdibs, a search engine for antiques, had already changed the interior design business in the States and was just altering the European design landscape.

Michael's taste for houses began at a very young age, when he became uber-successful investing in the real estate market in his hometown of San Francisco. Financial independence gave him the means and impetus to indulge his passion for other enterprises, as well as travel and design. A trip to a flea market in Paris is where he had his eureka moment—the idea that would turn him into a seminal player in the world of design. With infectious enthusiasm, he has brought new life to our industry.

Michael is an idea man and huge-hearted. On one of our trips together, he asked me to go clothes shopping, which I love to do. As he was piling up clothes ready to pay, he asked me what I was getting. I replied that I was on a money diet. "Oh, I hate being on that diet," he exclaimed. "Grab something, I'm buying!" That pretty much sums up his generosity and inclusive spirit. It is such a delight and a privilege to have him as a close friend.

My favorite rooms in the house are the mudroom and bar.

WHAT THINGS INSPIRE YOU THE MOST?

MOVIE? *Philadelphia Story.*

MUSIC? Baroque in the a.m., with coffee.

INTERIOR DESIGNER? Jean-Michel Frank.

ANTIQUE? 18th-century marquetry.

ARTIST? My sister, Sally Bruno.

BEACHES? The Hamptons.

FLOWER? Peony.

PLACE YOU'VE DISCOVERED OFF THE BEATEN PATH? Tuxedo Park, NY.

WHAT'S YOUR FAVORITE FILM? *Now, Voyager.*

WHAT ADVICE WOULD YOU GIVE TO PEOPLE BUYING THEIR FIRST HOUSE? Location, location, location.

IF YOU WEREN'T A BUSINESS ENTREPRENEUR, WHAT WOULD YOU DO? In my dreams, I am an architect.

DESCRIBE YOUR TYPICAL DAY. Coffee in bed with the newspaper at 6:30, dog walk on the property for an hour (we have 80 acres), e-mails and green juice, followed by a sporting activity—bike riding, yoga, tennis, and sometimes all three.

THREE ADJECTIVES THAT DESCRIBE YOU? Compulsive, optimistic, grateful.

The most important elements of a house are
PEOPLE AND PETS.

IF YOU WERE A COLOR WHAT WOULD YOU BE? Brown.

WHICH ERA WOULD YOU LIVE IN? 3000.

WHAT ARE YOUR BIGGEST PET PEEVES? When things are not put away where they belong, and waiting—I am very punctual.

WHERE ARE YOU MOST COMFORTABLE? Swimming in the ocean.

IF YOU COULD LIVE ANYWHERE, WHERE WOULD YOU RESIDE? Amalfi Coast.

WHAT'S YOUR GUILTY PLEASURE? Herbal relaxation.

WHOSE WORK DO YOU ADMIRE MOST? My mother's. She helps save immigrants that are crossing into the U.S. through the Arizona desert.

WHAT DO YOU LIKE ABOUT YOUR HOME? Important architecture and the view.

HOW OFTEN DOES YOUR HOME CHANGE? Way too often.

THE BEST PIECE OF ADVICE YOU HAVE EVER RECEIVED? Meditate and get more sleep. —Ariana Huffington

THE MOST COMMON MISTAKE PEOPLE MAKE? Jumping to conclusions.

"Work is more fun than fun."

—NOËL COWARD

INSPIRED BY . . .

» Perfect kitchen!

» Suspended over-counter shelving

» Mirror above the sink!

» Circular island

» Dark wood floors, window casements, and door

» Use of beadboard, different widths, some vertical, others horizontal

» Displaying books under the bed

DONNA DIXON AYKROYD

{ Regal Renaissance Lady }

I first met Donna and Danny at my wedding celebration in the mid-1980s. Since then, their friendship has been a reassuring constant of love, support, and joy.

So when I got the call that they were on the hunt for a new house, I was delighted to help them find it. Donna has a very specific, unerring eye, and her wish list for the property was challenging. Teaming up with my great friend and real estate guru Diane King, we scoured the L.A. market and pre-edited a list of presentable properties. For days the four of us crisscrossed the vast grid of L.A., traipsing through listings that ran the gamut from brand-new spec houses with sweeping views of the Pacific to Cliff May ranch homes shadowed by old-growth trees to expansive equestrian estates with rambling barns. But not one of them completely fit the bill. Diane got a last-minute call about a pocket listing, and so we braced ourselves for one more letdown but headed up into the Santa Monica Mountains anyway, giddy with exhaustion.

We entered the property through a nondescript gate into pure magic. The 1920s house had been built by an Italian diva as her summer getaway. The views were phenomenal, the gardens sprawling. Donna, a seasoned pro at house-hunting *and* a realist, was not looking to gut a house but did expect to have to make some renovations. But this property was literally turnkey. The former owners had meticulously restored it to its former glory.

I went on to help transition furniture from their previous house to the new one, and it was like Cinderella putting on the slipper. Everything fit perfectly. Both Donna and Danny knew immediately that it was home.

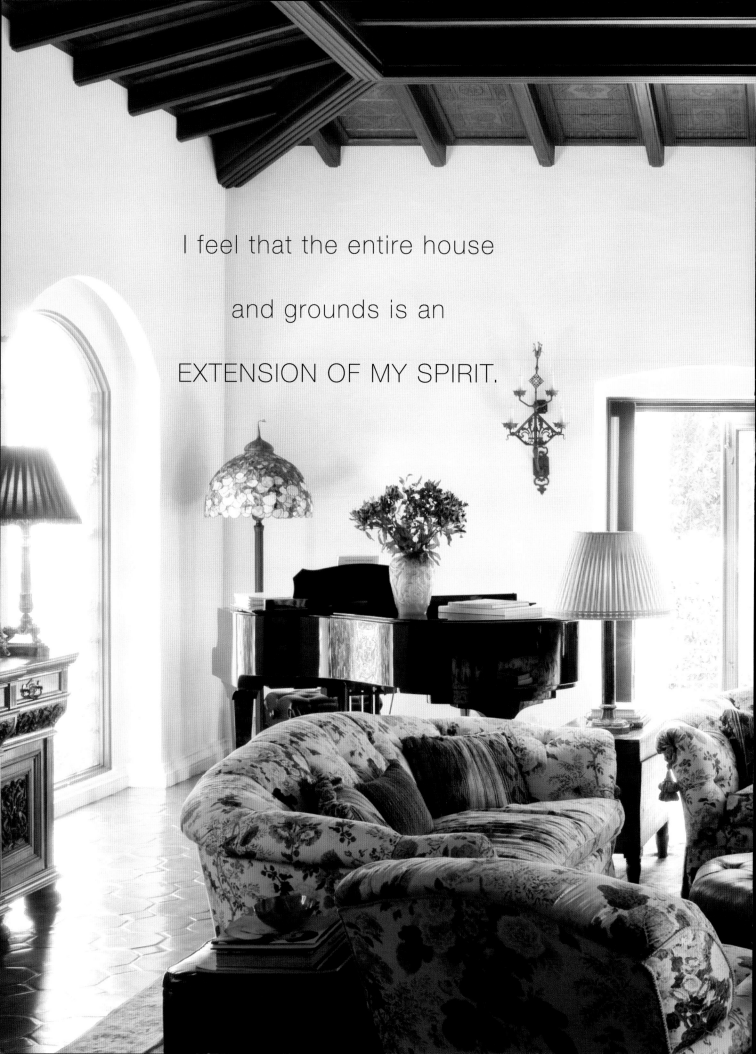

I feel that the entire house

and grounds is an

EXTENSION OF MY SPIRIT.

WHAT INSPIRES YOU MOST? My family, classical architecture, food, music, and inner beauty.

WHAT IS YOUR FAVORITE MOVIE? I can't pick just one: *Mr. Smith Goes to Washington, Gladiator, The Third Man, The Day the Earth Stood Still, Dr. Strangelove.*

YOUR FAVORITE BOOK? The best book I've read recently is *The River of Doubt.*

FAVORITE QUOTE? "Never for me the lowered banner, never the last endeavor." —Ernest Shackleton

A COMMON MISTAKE PEOPLE MAKE? Judging a book by its cover.

ADVICE FOR PEOPLE BUYING THEIR FIRST HOUSE? Location, sound geological assessment, property taxes.

WHAT THREE THINGS COULD YOU NOT LIVE WITHOUT? My family, my library, and my vintage belt that I've worn everywhere: tracking tigers in India, traveling to the bottom of the world to research climate change in Antarctica, and observing polar bears in the wilds of Manitoba.

WHAT'S THE MOST INTERESTING THING YOU HAVE EVER FOUND? The skull of a Pachyrhinosaurus on a paleontological dig in Alberta, Canada.

DESCRIBE YOURSELF WITH THREE ADJECTIVES. Adventurous, positive, and compassionate.

WHAT DO YOU COLLECT? French impressionist art; nudes. When I was younger I collected cast-iron architectural coin banks.

WHAT ARE YOUR BIGGEST PET PEEVES? Laziness, ignorance, and dishonesty.

YOUR CHILDHOOD OBSESSION? Growing up in DC, the National Art Gallery was my haunt.

HOW OFTEN DOES YOUR HOME CHANGE? The energy of the home stays the same, but I'm always working to make it the best it can possibly be. I work in the garden tending roses, planting fruit trees. We recently added an outdoor breakfast terrace and herb garden off the kitchen, overlooking the mountains. My next project is to begin cultivating orchids.

What's really special about my home is its spiritual energy. I awake very early because I love to walk the grounds in the quiet of the morning. It's like being in a monastery.

INSPIRED BY . . .

» Period wrought iron and tile work

» European influence—vintage chintzes, artwork, and lighting

» Tiffany lamps

» Proportion and scale of furnishings

» Capacious sofas and chairs, make comfort premium

» Curved wall of French doors in the master suite

» Celebrates indoor/outdoor lifestyle of California

» Relationship to outdoors as important as the décor

» Labyrinth garden design creates beautiful secret havens

BABY DE SELLIERS

{ The Equestrian }

My first encounter with Baby occurred in my Santa Monica living room, and my first impression was that she was languid, lethargic, and low-key. It didn't take long to realize that she is anything but! She just happened to be depressed after breaking up with her latest boyfriend.

Our friendship really evolved when Baby found a stable block just north of Sunset Boulevard with a 1950s ranch-style Cliff May-esque house attached. She bought the property primarily for the stables, but the house had good enough bones—and who doesn't want to sleep with the sound of baying horses in their ear? My brother Robert managed the renovation, opening up walls and making the house livable.

A genuine eccentric to the core, Baby rolls right off the pages of a Mitford novel; she was definitely British in a past life. Her love of horses (she has twelve in her backyard) and her years spent in London make her more English than most of my fellow "teabags."

Though I think *eclectic* is so overused, it applies perfectly to Baby. The way she haphazardly puts things together is inimitable: a stuffed squirrel running up the living room wall, a toy tiger in the bookcase, a boar's head in the dining room, and walls crammed with her own paintings: portraits of dogs, people, and birds. Everything about Baby is delightfully childlike, starting with her name, which is rumored to have been dreamt up in the hospital because her mother couldn't think what else to call her. Baby is the consummate entertainer. There is always a lamb slow-cooking in the oven and a bottle of tequila on the drinks table ready to be poured. And there is always laughter—mainly her own overpowering everyone else's.

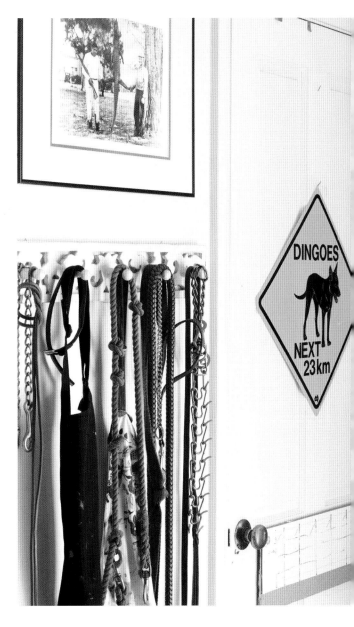

WHO IS YOUR FAVORITE ARCHITECT? Tom Kundig. He can make a house come right out of rock.

FAVORITE PLACES? Scotland and the San Juan Islands.

IF YOU WEREN'T A PAINTER, WHAT WOULD YOU BE? I'd like to be a hairdresser.

WHAT ARE YOUR PET PEEVES? Stinginess, insecurity, and lack of curiosity.

WHAT DO YOU COLLECT? Starfish and wishbones and gold.

FAVORITE MOVIES? The best ones are about secrets and lies, especially with beautiful young people. And the endurance of wonder and innocence.

I've always been obsessed with PIRATES AND HORSES, so as children we were gangs of pirates galloping our ponies everywhere.

I AM INSPIRED MOST by *my family*, friends, cooking, eating and drinking together; *dancing and music; and* whatever I'm smelling.

FAVORITE QUOTES

"You and I have brains. The others have fluff."

—RABBIT, FROM *THE HOUSE AT POOH CORNER*

"Boldness has genius, power, and magic in it." —GOETHE

MY FAVORITE COLOR IS WHITE, like an invitation, a baker's smock, a man's handkerchief, a christening gown. White sheets and white socks.

BUY BIG

if you are

buying a

house.

INSPIRED BY . . .

» Collections of ordinary things

» The traditional juxtaposed with the unusual—
pigs on a chandelier

» Toile, floral, and paisley fabrics in the living
room—nothing matches, yet it all does

» Lampshade fabric *mine!*

» Walls of paintings

» Dog portraits

» Drawers in dressing room hand-painted by
Baby with whimsical designs

» Everything reflects Baby

» Nothing is dull

CARINA COOPER

{ Colorful Chef/Writer }

When you walk into any of Carina's homes, you know immediately that you have arrived someplace extraordinarily special. We met in our early teens at a birthday party in Gloucestershire. Carina grew up nearby in one of the most beautiful houses in England, which dates back to Elizabethan times. Our formative years were similar. We both spent our early twenties in New York, when the disco culture of Studio 54 and Xenon was all the rage, then went on to Los Angeles, where we both married film directors and started our families. It was Carina who fell in love with the French countryside and advised me to buy a rundown pile anywhere south of the Dordogne.

Carina's taste has always been colorful, imaginative, and impeccable. Her first flat in Notting Hill was done with such style—Boho chic (way before the phrase was coined) meets the California flea market. She was wildly ahead of her time—influenced by Mexican and Western style way before any of us—and her singular style has continued to inspire all of her friends to this day.

Carina possesses an amazing ability to find unique properties. From Hollywood to Notting Hill to the Devon countryside, she creates magic. In the next few pages we visit her farm in Devon. She brings Moroccan textiles and French antiques to the English countryside and, as with her cooking, she knows how to marry unconventional ingredients to create something original and fabulous.

IF YOU WEREN'T A WRITER, WHAT WOULD YOU BE? An acrobat.

IF YOU COULD LIVE IN ANY ERA? It would be the 1940s.

IN YOUR NEXT LIFE, WHAT WOULD YOU LIKE TO BE? I'd come back as one of the swallows from my barn who makes such a heroic journey from Devon to Africa and back again in a year.

I COLLECT

bird nests,

pebbles,

anything

FROM

NATURE.

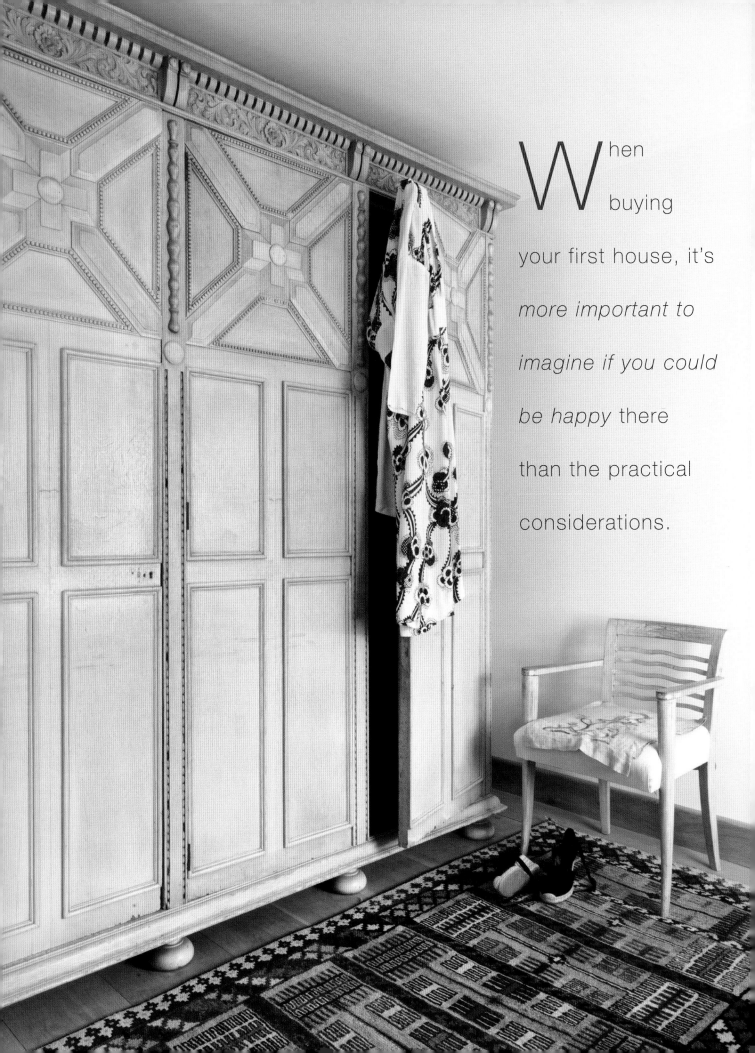

When buying your first house, it's *more important to imagine if you could be happy* there than the practical considerations.

WHAT INSPIRES YOU?

ART? Folk art.

COUNTRY? France.

ANIMAL? Horses.

CULTURE? Mexican.

WHAT PERIOD ANTIQUES DO YOU LIKE? French 1940s.

ARTIST? Turner.

FLOWERS? Apple blossoms.

PLACE YOU'VE DISCOVERED OFF THE BEATEN PATH? Ulpotha, Sri Lanka.

FAVORITE BOOK? *Adventures in Contentment* by David Grayson. (I found an original 1860s issue with a red suede cover in a secondhand bookstore.)

YOUR CHILDHOOD OBSESSIONS? Flea markets and making shampoo from dried herbs.

MUSIC YOU'VE REDISCOVERED? Led Zeppelin's "Ramble On." (I do my housework to it).

MY FAVORITE ROOM

in the house is

WHICHEVER ONE I'M IN.

NATURE inspires

me most.

INSPIRED BY . . .

» Paint color—bright and bold

» Use of textiles—exotic ethnic cloth,
  tribal weavings, vintage European

» Combining old and new—Mid-
  century modern and British Arts and
  Crafts with French country

» Attention to detail—Greek textiles
  appliquéd onto plain linens

» Lacquered woodwork

» Bookcases made from wood scaffolding planks

» Books arranged by color block

» Artwork on shelves

» Use of a folding screen/room divider as a headboard

» Tables piled with potted geraniums (and I'm not much of an indoor
  plant person)

RAY AZOULAY

{ Magician }

Ray's legendary shop in Venice, Obsolete, was my obsession way before Ray himself was. It is one of the handful of places I insist my European friends visit when in Los Angeles. It's divinely theatrical, ever-changing, and refreshingly original—quite like Ray himself.

Everything about Ray is unexpected, but let's start with his wardrobe. To say he likes to mix it up is an understatement. He could be dressed as an old-fashioned tradesman from a French hardware store one day, a symphony conductor another time, and a Cirque du Soleil acrobat the next. Ray is not only one of the most highly regarded antiques dealers in L.A., but in the past few years he has earned a reputation as one of the city's leading art curators as well.

Unlike Obsolete, Ray's home is quiet and discreet. Once you walk up the stairs past a bakery, you enter a serene realm where the bright candy chaos of Venice Beach fades away. The layout is organized around a private central courtyard, so it's all about light and open space. The furnishings are minimal and the palette neutral, creating a chic Spartan vibe. And everything is *something*. But if you're looking for color, you'll have to open one of Ray's closets.

The artwork is very much a focus of Ray's living space, and the lack of superfluous furnishings and objects is compensated by the presence of light streaming in from every direction. You can not only see the sea but also feel its powerful rhythms. It might be Ray's house, but, to me, it has the restorative energy of a secluded retreat.

EVERYONE should spend an hour sitting in

IF YOU WERE AN ANIMAL, WHAT WOULD YOU BE? An elephant.

IF YOU COULD LIVE ANYWHERE, ANYTIME? I've always wanted to live on the moon, or in the Victorian Era.

THREE ADJECTIVES THAT DESCRIBE YOU? Discerning, judgmental, and more judgmental.

IN YOUR NEXT LIFE, WHO WOULD YOU LIKE TO BE? A superhero who can fly.

FAVORITE MOVIES? A range of movies, from *Blue Jasmine* to *Terms of Endearment.* I love the part where Shirley MacLaine loses it in the ICU.

MUSIC? Max Richter's recomposed *Vivaldi, The Four Seasons.*

YOUR ART AND DESIGN INSPIRATIONS? Irving Penn photographs; John Pawson; Michaël Borremans; Rei Kawakubo.

WHAT THINGS INSPIRE YOU?

PLACE? London.

DOG? Irish wolfhound.

FLOWER? Long-stemmed white French tulip.

ANTIQUE? Primitive Windsor chair.

BOOK? The dictionary.

CULTURE? Italian.

FAVORITE RESTAURANT? Any good diner where
the coffee keeps coming.

THE THREE THINGS YOU CANNOT LIVE WITHOUT? Hair creme from Kiehl's, good shoes, and my vintage MBZ.

WHAT'S YOUR TYPICAL DAY LIKE? Lots of laughing.

MY HOME CHANGES *EVERY* 15 MINUTES.

INSPIRED BY . . .

» Interior courtyard

» Light and use of glass

» Concrete floors with area rugs

» Primary artists on the walls

» Wall of wood in the master from Alice Tully Hall at Lincoln Center

» Classic Fortuny-inspired wallpaper

» The unexpected

» Sense of humor

» Juxtaposition of architecture and furnishings

» Nothing is boring!

LADY ANNABEL GOLDSMITH

{ Grand Dame }

The first person of my parents' generation that I was able to call by her Christian name was Annabel. An iconic figure, passionate mother and grandmother, author, and traveler (only to hot climates), she is a purveyor of great English taste. Born to the 8th Marquess of Londonderry and married to Mark Birley, she is without doubt one of the most fun and generous people in my life. She grew up in great splendor between Wynyard Park, County Durham, and at Londonderry House, Park Lane, where she had her coming out party.

I was in awe of her taste and spent many an afternoon listening to Annabel's stories, surrounded by her dogs, family, and endless friends, howling with laughter. We still laugh over my mother's phone calls to her, asking her to insist that I get myself a bra that fit properly!

The Queen Anne house in Richmond, Surrey, which she and her late husband, Sir James Goldsmith, moved to in the mid-'70s, was designed by a young Nina Campbell and Tom Parr of Colefax and Fowler. Many of the rooms remain the same as they were forty years ago; the chintz master bedroom has elegantly stood the test of time. When the fabrics were looking a bit worn out, I recall Annabel asking me what to do next. I said, "The same; it doesn't get much better than this."

When I launched my first fabric collection in 1997, Annabel very generously gave me a guest bedroom to redecorate in order to feature my designs. Her generosity, love of life, and sense of style continue to inspire me.

WHAT ADVICE WOULD YOU GIVE SOMEONE BUYING A HOUSE? Make sure it's where you want to be and analyze how it compares to the one you are leaving.

THREE THINGS YOU CAN'T LIVE WITHOUT? Dogs, books, and my grandchildren.

FAVORITE FILMS? I equally love *Gone with the Wind* and *All about Eve.*

YOUR FAVORITE COLOR? Pink.

WHICH ERA WOULD YOU LIKED TO HAVE LIVED IN? Early Edwardian (don't like the architecture, though) or to have been in the court of Charles II.

YOUR PET PEEVES? Bad manners and lateness.

FAVORITE ANIMAL? Horses.

WHAT IS YOUR GUILTY PLEASURE? Eating sweets!

IF YOU WERE TO PLAY OPPOSITE AN ACTOR, WHO WOULD IT BE? Either Liam Neeson or Denzel Washington.

DO YOU PREFER SUNRISE OR SUNSET? Sunrise.

FAVORITE PIECE OF ART TO OWN? Anything by Alma-Tadema or Stubbs.

WHAT KIND OF MUSIC DO YOU LIKE? Classical or music from the '60s.

"There is only one thing in the world worse than being talked about, and that is not being talked about." —OSCAR WILDE

My guest bedroom was rather spooky owing to the old legend of the murder that took place there in the 18th century. Then Kathryn came to the rescue and transformed it by use of her vibrant colors into one of the prettiest and coziest rooms in the house.

INSPIRED BY . . .

» Egg yolk-striated library

» Painted paneled walls

» Upholstered walls

» Walls filled with paintings

» Children's art on walls alongside old masters

» Hidden doors

» Florals with bullion fringe

» Colefax and Fowler chintz all over the master bedroom

» Floor-to-ceiling windows

» Authentic architecture

» Family history

MIV WATTS

{ The Decorating Rock Chick }

Some years ago, Miv walked onto my stand at Decorex (London's interior design show) and in her wonderful "Miv" way told me how much she loved my textiles and that she used them in her design work. Loving a compliment, I became her fast friend. We have much in common. Miv divides her time between the South of France and Los Angeles. Her daughter, Naomi, is virtually a neighbor. She has a wicked sense of humor; her stories of life in the music business during the '70s are wildly enthralling; her lack of formality and inherent good taste make her the perfect traveling and antiquing companion.

Miv lives during the summer months with her two whippets and a part-time Old Etonian fishmonger at a part 14th-, part 18th-century silk factory in the heart of Saint-Hippolyte-du-Fort, close to Montpellier and the Mediterranean Sea. Her favorite room is the *salon* on the first floor of her town house, in which she has been able to effortlessly incorporate the three things she requires to convert a house into a home: comfort, color, and history. This fabulous room also features a pair of grand old post office doors.

Outdoor patios connect various rooms in the multistoried house. She is a savvy collector of anything and everything, but what she looks for in an object are humor and juxtaposition possibilities. Her biggest regret (she thinks about this missed opportunity daily) was not buying thirty life-size penguins—a tiny army of hilarious waiters!

138

My house is a constant work in progress.

WHERE DO YOU LIKE TO BUY FURNITURE? The three major antique fairs in the south are Montpellier, Avignon, and Beziers—all on my doorstep. Otherwise, it's India; I'm obsessed with India.

YOUR INSPIRATIONS? Travel and antique textiles.

WHAT DO YOU MOST LIKE ABOUT YOUR HOME? I like the theater of it. It's an ever-changing set. I can let things go and am forever gathering more things, depending on what character I am playing out in my head.

Salt

Rice

Coffee

Paste

Sugar

HOME

ESSENTIALS?

A comfortable

bed, a serious

wet room,

outdoor space

for eating,

and oodles of

fabulous light.

mportant things to have in your home: dogs, fresh market produce, a long refectory table, and as many fragrant flowers as the season will allow.

My home never changes; it's just a *movable feast,* a circus. It all depends ON WHAT PARTICULAR act one walks into.

INSPIRED BY . . .

» Australian, Indian, French, English

» Use of color

» Bloomsbury art

» Tile work

» Layering of textures

» The informality of the rooms

» Brick and plaster work combined

» Well-edited accessories

» Boho chic

Life's too short to be
ANYTHING but AUTHENTIC.

FIONA LEWIS

{ The Natural }

Fiona Lewis and her husband, Art Linson, a well-known Hollywood producer, became two of my great friends when I first moved to Los Angeles. When in town, a week doesn't go by that we don't meet for dinner or drop by each other's houses. We are like family and are now neighbors on two continents—in Santa Monica and southern France.

Fiona grew up in England but moved to California in her twenties. She is a world-class friend, dinner companion, and traveling pal. She is a journalist, novelist, and screenwriter. She loves all things French, in particular Directoire furniture and the Quercy countryside. With no formal interior design training and only herself as a client, she routinely prowls California flea markets looking for original Bauer pottery, '40s Lucite candlesticks, and vintage Taxco silver jewelry. In France, where passion for browsing the brocantes, flea markets, and antique shops is a way of life, Fiona fits right in. She has an infallible eye for combining the timeless and the chic with a contemporary twist for knockout results.

Art and Fiona's beach-side home in Santa Monica has the bones of the last century, but the sensibility of her interior decor is very now. Fiona's passion for mixing eras is evident with a well-curated collection of furniture that includes pieces by Noguchi, Eames, Frankl, Rohde, and Wright. Paintings by local Venice artists and friends animate wall space all over the house.

As a couple, Art and Fiona encompass traits that make them a perfect team: wit, beauty, and above all, great taste.

WHAT IS YOUR TYPICAL DAY LIKE? In the morning I do the minimum exercise possible, then I go to my office and write. I stay there, welcoming interruptions, until I can't take it anymore. Then I read the newspapers, have a vodka, and think about making dinner.

YOUR GUILTY PLEASURES? Buying furniture, reading, and traveling—all of which remove me from the tedium of reality.

WHAT DO YOU COLLECT? Rohde furniture, Russell Wright china, and James Perse T-shirts.

THE BEST PIECE OF ADVICE YOU HAVE RECEIVED? From my husband—and this applies to almost everything, but in particular decorating: "There are no mistakes and everything can be fixed."

WHAT INSPIRES YOU THE MOST? Other people's talents.

FAVORITE QUOTE? Flaubert's "Be regular and orderly in your life . . . so that you may be violent and original in your work." I feel, however, that I have failed the orderly part.

WHAT WAS YOUR CHILDHOOD OBSESSION? Dragging in large pieces of trees from our garden and putting them in vases.

I CAN'T LIVE WITHOUT expensive
sheets, homemade mayonnaise,
and my husband.

THE MOST IMPORTANT ELEMENTS IN A HOUSE are a sense of *space, light, and airiness.*

Large rooms and as many windows as possible.

My favorite room in the house is the bathroom. I am a girl from
the '60s, after all, when most of the fun took place there.

INSPIRED BY . . .

» French and Moroccan influences

» A floor plan that flows effortlessly between public and private rooms

» Maple woodwork

» Bright, colorful abstract artwork

» The Hockney portrait of Celia Birtwell

» Exterior paint color—light taupe with off-white trim

» Poul Henningsen light fixture in kitchen

» Forties influence in every room

MARTYN
LAWRENCE BULLARD

{ Design Star }

Martyn is one of those rare people whose mere presence arrives way before he does! His gorgeous mellifluous voice is almost indistinct from his laughter. They are melded together as one.

Martyn's landmark house, previously owned by iconic twenties film star Gloria Swanson, is located in a Hollywood neighborhood renowned as one of the earliest celebrity enclaves. The entry to the Mediterranean-style villa is reminiscent of a Moroccan *riad* and, once you've stepped all the way in, the romance with the house never ends. Spending a day in his home, I was really able to appreciate all the detail, from the staircase railings to the inset tile work to the hand-painted mural on the dining room ceiling. It reminded me of my own house, only better!

Martyn is one of the most handsome men I know, so it's no surprise that he came to Hollywood to pursue a career as an actor. But before long, his good taste got the better of him and he became not a movie star himself but the most sought-after interior designer to the stars. His gift is to interpret and incorporate design idioms in a unique style that is balanced, intelligent, and boldly confident. He has been a beloved friend and huge support as a fellow designer and a cast member of our two-season Bravo show, *Million Dollar Decorators*.

Irreverence, charm, and hard work are the three character traits I admire most, and Martyn has them all.

TRAVEL INSPIRES ME THE MOST OF EVERYTHING IN MY LIFE. The colors, smells, tastes of a new place are always exciting, but when mixed with a new culture and the sights that go with that, all my decorative juices flow like Niagara Falls. My work is totally infused with the kaleidoscope of ideas my travels have afforded me. It's my internal library.

WHAT ROLE WOULD YOU LIKE TO PLAY IN A MOVIE? I would play Oscar Wilde in a movie if only I could pull off that extraordinary wit. And *Auntie Mame,* of course, is my favorite movie, for both the ever-revolving decorating scenes and the campy humor. Delicious entertainment.

WHAT COLOR WOULD YOU BE? Paloma Picasso red—fiery, sexy, yet sophisticated when I feel like it!

FAVORITE TIME PERIOD? I would live in the Roaring Twenties, a decadent decade with frivolous fashions, deifying design, and fascinating artists.

WHAT IS YOUR FAVORITE ROOM IN YOUR HOUSE? My tiny screening room. I love movies and like to watch them in there, cuddled up with my dog, under a cashmere blanket with a glass of wine. It's my sanctuary— what more can I say!

DO YOU LIKE SUNRISES OR SUNSETS? Sunsets. I'm not a good morning person, so I always miss sunrises, unless I've had a particularly wild evening, and then the sunrise seems so naughtily amusing.

I always wanted
to be a singer,
so in my next life
I want to perform
for thousands,
or even for a few,
as long as they get
lost in my voice
and the melodic
tales I will croon to
them.

THE MOST IMPORTANT ELEMENT OF A HOUSE,

for me, is the lighting. It can make or break an ambiance,

and a home is not a home without it. Design tip number one:

invest in dimmer switches for every room, even the loo!

INSPIRED BY . . .

» A riot of cultures—Indian, Mexican, Moroccan, and European

» Large patterns with small prints

» Religious art

» Use of black and white—nobody does it better!

» Preference for candlelight

» Pair of oversized mirrors from Martyn's collection

» European-height dining table with large armchairs

» Candlesticks repurposed as lamps

Best piece of advice received was

"BELIEVE IN YOURSELF AND YOUR TALENT,

THEN OTHERS WILL BELIEVE IN YOU TOO."

And so was born my career.

CHRISTOPHER FARR

{ Color Enthusiast }

Walking into Chris's studio in Santa Monica one is immediately and happily overwhelmed by glorious carpet art. Apart from his collection of Moroccan and Middle Eastern rugs, all the other carpets are designed by Chris and they are breathtaking. Because the space was designed first and foremost as an artist's studio, and then a home, there's a refreshing informality to the environment. There is no pretense; just the feeling of a man doing what he loves. Everything else is afterthought. To me, there is nothing more attractive than a man who is not afraid of color and knows how to use it.

I've known Christopher for many years, since he had his first shop in Notting Hill, a charming and unpretentious operation that served a small but incredibly loyal clientele. For a while, Chris was the best-kept secret in London, but when he moved to L.A. with his family and opened a flagship store in West Hollywood's design district, my "insider" fan status was over. Now everybody knows about him. And so they should. His rugs are phenomenal. The Bauhaus movement is clearly an influence on Christopher's designs, as are silent movies, the monumental beauty of Louis Kahn buildings, and the dramatic landscapes of Scotland. Most recently, he acquired the rights to the Bloomsbury Group's work. I'm eager to see what results.

What I

like most

about my

home is

its size.

WHAT INSPIRES YOU? Silent movies, Peter Sellers in *The Party;* Bauhaus.

WHAT ARTISTS DO YOU MOST ADMIRE? Alighiero Boetti, Alexander Calder, and William Segal.

WHAT PLACES DO YOU DRAW INSPIRATION FROM? Scotland, Istanbul, and the beaches at Barafundle, Wales.

WHAT THREE THINGS COULD YOU NOT LIVE WITHOUT? Living Tea, Nairn's biscuits, Netflix.

WHO WOULD PLAY YOU IN A MOVIE? Donald Sutherland in *Don't Look Now.*

IF YOU COULD LIVE IN ANY ERA, WHICH WOULD IT BE? Paris in the 1930s.

IF YOU COULD HAVE ANY PAINTING, WHICH ONE WOULD YOU HANG IN YOUR ENTRY FOYER? *The Stonemason's Yard,* Canaletto.

WHAT'S THE MOST INTERESTING THING YOU'VE EVER FOUND? A section of the audience carpet of Shah Jahangir, the Mughal emperor whose son built the Taj Mahal.

IF YOU COULD PLAY OPPOSITE ANY ACTOR, WHO WOULD IT BE? Tina Fey.

When buying a house,

spend more than you want to

IF YOU LOVE IT.

INSPIRED BY . . .

» Using the bathroom wall as a pinboard

» A nook for a kitchen

» Having brushes and canvases right there, for working day or night

» Everything is captivating

» Layering carpets

URSULA BROOKS

{ The Comedian }

Ursula is my most hilarious friend. A trained actress from Sydney whose forte is comedy and impersonations, she plays me almost better than me! We met some years ago when my Australian assistant suddenly had to leave the States, and like all good Aussies, Ursula came on board to help me finish a design job. When we're both in California, we talk often and take walks in the Santa Monica Mountains.

We have taken many trips together. One was for a house installation in Normandy, France, where the clients decided to arrive a day earlier than planned. Disaster. The cleaners never showed up; the furniture was still in transit from Paris; and Urs and I woke up late due to a few too many glasses of rosé and me breaking up with my boyfriend at 1 a.m.—let's just say the house was *tres dishabille!*

Ursula lives in a charming Spanish house in Brentwood, California, with actor Jonathan LaPaglia and their delightful daughter, Tilly. The easiest error to make when remodeling a house is to take away its soul. What inspires me the most about Ursula: even though she took her 1920s house down to the studs, she maintained the architectural integrity of the original structure and the period aesthetics. The rooms flow effortlessly into each other and then into nature. She has brilliantly converted her garden into a splendid outdoor living room, and the kitchen opens up onto a wide veranda that can serve as a dining room. Concertina doors over the counter remain open all day long, allowing the scent of oranges and lavender to waft throughout the house. It was this garden that really inspired me when I finally packed up the boys' trampoline and relandscaped my own grounds.

LOOK AT THE BONES OF THE HOUSE.
I personally would *not* go for something
that has "BEEN DONE," as in redone.

IF YOU COULD LIVE IN ANY ERA, WHEN WOULD IT BE? Definitely the '20s in Berlin or Paris. It was such an era of celebration and artistic inspiration. The party scene was so incredibly chic and daring.

WHAT ARE YOUR BIGGEST PET PEEVES? Bad manners, bad breath, brown bananas, and stingy people.

WHERE ARE YOU MOST COMFORTABLE? In my own home. I absolutely *love* being there.

IF YOU COULD HAVE ANY PAINTING, WHICH ONE WOULD YOU HANG IN YOUR ENTRY FOYER? *La Classe de Danse* by Edgar Degas.

IF MONEY WERE NO OBJECT, WHAT WOULD YOU BUY? I would get my own private jet, then I could go anywhere and see everything and throw friends on board as well. Heaven!

HOW DO YOU SEE YOURSELF? I've always thought of myself as thoughtful, tortured, and loving.

IF YOU COULD LIVE ANYWHERE, WHERE WOULD IT BE? I'd move to Italy, somewhere in Umbria or Tuscany or by the sea.

IF YOU COULD PLAY OPPOSITE ANY ACTOR, WHO WOULD IT BE? George Clooney. Doesn't he have a house in Italy?

big kitchen that can open onto the backyard is essential, and it should face the sunset. I would also put energy into good bathrooms; you spend more time in there than you think.

INSPIRED BY . . .

» Religious objects as art pieces

» Dedicated TV room

» Kitchen that opens onto the terrace, with bifold doors above sink

» Using large-scale pieces in small rooms

» Tropical plants

» Mexican/Moroccan/Australian vibe

» Colored walls

» Great use of small spaces

My mother taught me to LOVE MANY, trust but few, learn to PADDLE YOUR OWN CANOE.

ADAM BLACKMAN

{ Historian }

Adam has been in the antiques business for as long as I've lived here—twenty-five years or so. In 1993, Adam and his business partner, David Cruz, opened Blackman Cruz on La Cienega Boulevard, which quickly became legendary as the ultimate emporium for furniture and décor in Los Angeles. It has since moved to Highland Avenue, to a location that once served as a gay after-hours club.

This man, who started out with a stall at the Santa Monica Antique Market, is now widely acknowledged as one of the top dealers in the world. Adam has such a trained eye and appreciation for excellence that over the years he has amassed singular collections of museum-quality ceramics, pottery, and furniture.

Whether bumping into Adam and his fabulous wife, Kate, a graphic designer, in an airport or at a flea market, infectious laughter always ensues. There is something almost innocent about Adam's uninhibited enthusiasm for his design passion, which is apparent on entering their house in Brentwood, California. This mid-century modern gem, designed by A. Quincy Jones, is a masterpiece tucked away in the trees but with a 180-degree view of the Santa Monica Mountains. The house is full of rare pieces of furniture by Giò Ponti, Billy Haines, Paul Frankl, and Fritz Hansen.

Adam is a bon vivant, so I wasn't surprised to learn that his three favorite things are eating, shopping, and eating!

The most important
element of a house
is natural light.

YOUR FAVORITE ARTIST? Rembrandt Bugatti.

PLACE YOU'VE DISCOVERED OFF THE BEATEN PATH? Villa Necchi Campiglio, in Milan.

PERSON? My grandmother, Rose Moses.

SINGER/MUSICIAN? Billy Joel.

BOOK? *The Last Lecture,* by Randy Pausch.

WHAT THREE THINGS COULD YOU NOT LIVE WITHOUT? Ivory soap, my automaton collection, and my family.

WHO WOULD PLAY YOU IN A MOVIE? Don Knotts.

WHAT ANIMAL WOULD YOU BE? An otter.

IF YOU COULD LIVE ANYWHERE, WHERE WOULD YOU RESIDE? The Met.

IF YOU WEREN'T AN ANTIQUE AND FURNITURE DEALER, WHAT WOULD YOU DO? I'd be a lounge singer.

THREE ADJECTIVES THAT DESCRIBE YOU? Sarcastic, clean, hardworking.

WHAT COLOR WOULD YOU BE? Orange.

FAVORITE QUOTE? "You'll worry less about what people think about you when you realize how seldom they do." —David Foster Wallace

YOUR BIGGEST PET PEEVE? Carelessness.

WHAT INSPIRES YOU?

MOVIE? *The Diving Bell and the Butterfly.*

COUNTRY? Israel.

ARCHITECT? John Lautner.

ANIMAL? Uncle Leo (our cat).

CITY? New York.

RESTAURANT? Fifteen, in London.

ANTIQUE? Anything by Carlo Bugatti.

WHEN ARE YOU MOST COMFORTABLE? Sundays at home.

IN YOUR NEXT LIFE, WHO WOULD LIKE TO BE? A prosecuting attorney.

WHAT PAINTING WOULD YOU LIKE TO HANG IN YOUR ENTRY FOYER? Anything by de Chirico.

WHAT'S YOUR GUILTY PLEASURE? Staying in nice hotels.

IF MONEY WERE NO OBJECT, WHAT WOULD YOU SPLURGE ON? A full-time driver.

ANYWHERE my wife and the cats are IS HOME.

I like that my home is surrounded by trees.

INSPIRED BY . . .

- » Diverse collections, from 60 AD to present day

- » Orange partition wall dividing up spaces

- » Using color minimally, making a big impact

- » Glass, wood, and cement

- » Architecture not overshadowed by furnishings

- » Louvered panels create intimate spaces

GABY DELLAL

{ Triple Threat }

I first met Gaby—a director, writer, actress—on the 5:55 pm to Gillingham, on my way to spend the weekend with my best friend Cosima at her mother's fabulous house in Somerset. We were twelve; I had finished my first term at Heathfield, Ascot, the sister school to Eton. There was Gaby, wearing French Connection skinny tight red velvet jeans, the epitome of grooviness, as far as I was concerned. Although it was the '70s, London was not over the '60s by any means—or at least Kids in Gear on The King's Road was where it was at.

Gaby's first house in Notting Hill Gate, I remember so well. From a young age, she has had a preternaturally sophisticated sense of how to put things together, whether it was her tight jeans and a statement top, or a Kurdistan textile flung on the back of a sofa, or a Moorish carpet thrown on the wall as art. Gaby is *never not* an inspiration. She has designed as many interiors as most professional decorators, including a brownstone in New York, a residence in Islington, a cottage in Cornwall, and now a revamp of her own Notting Hill place, which has been home base to Gaby and her three boys for many years. Unlike most London houses built on narrow urban lots, hers is a wide structure that spans the breadth of the street. And thanks to all that extra space, my three boys and I always have a place to call home in London, just as she and her three boys always have a home with us in L.A.

Gaby's design hallmarks—innovative use of color, philosophy of space, and sense of dimension—are incomparable and always inspiring.

The kitchen is the MOST IMPORTANT ROOM in the house.

WHAT DO YOU COLLECT? Plates by Hylton Nel.

WHERE DO YOU CONSIDER HOME? London, and I wouldn't want to live anywhere else.

FAVORITE FILMS? This year, *Dallas Buyers Club* and *Her*.

YOUR FAVORITE DRINKS? Coffee and wine.

MUSIC? Bluegrass.

ARTIST? Calder.

CULTURE? South America.

ARCHITECT? Oscar Niemeyer.

ANIMALS? Dogs and horses.

CITY? New York.

PLACE OFF THE BEATEN PATH? Garzón, Uruguay.

FAVORITE BEACH? Chapel Porth, Cornwall.

BIRD? The goldfinch.

When buying YOUR FIRST HOUSE, remember

that it's not just a house, IT'S A HOME.

INSPIRED BY . . .

» Use of space

» Wall paint color in living room with furniture, purple paint with silver furniture

» Ability to take old and make contemporary

» Pops of color

» Neon sign as art

» Pinning canvases on the wall— frameless

» Always the unexpected. Conventional photo of her son turned to the side

» Boldness—hanging the bikes in hallway to become objects

» Modern-day toile in guest bedroom

» Using a flag as a window treatment

WINDSOR SMITH

{ Design 411 }

Windsor and I first met at "Mummy and Me" with our sons Otis (mine) and Trinity (hers). As we sat in "the circle" singing "Wheels on the Bus," we caught each other's eye. The look was mutual. Are we really here? And so our friendship began. At that time, I was a mother of three boys under the age of four. I had a small shop selling English housewares and textiles, and Windsor was roaming the highways and byways of California sourcing antiques and vintage furnishings. One winter I decamped to France with my boys to work on the renovation of my recently purchased farmhouse and I got a call from Windsor. In her pronounced Texas accent, she told me she was in France at a place called Gaillac, pronouncing it just that way, "Gaylack," as you would expect. Of course, I only knew it as "Guy-ack." It took us a few moments to realize that she was virtually at my doorstep.

When I went into interior design, which was right about then, Windsor's shop became one of my go-to destinations. She has an extraordinary eye, blending old farm paraphernalia with Directoire, George III, and Portuguese antiques. Some years later, when both of our lives were subsumed by our careers and marshaling teenage boys, I was looking through some fabric invoices and noticed there seemed to be a lot from Windsor Smith. Impulsively, I picked up the phone and invited her to come right over. What I forgot to tell her was that I would be taking her to the beach to do kettlebells!

Windsor is full of life, smart as a whip, and generous to a fault. She is in constant motion unless you arrive at the end of the day, when she has put her work to bed and is reclining on a chaise by the pool.

WHEN BUYING

your first house,

buy something that

you can afford to

MAKE YOUR OWN.

YOUR FAVORITE BOOKS? *The Great Gatsby, The Quiet Answer.*

FAVORITE QUOTE? "Smile! It increases your face value." —*Steel Magnolias.*

DESCRIBE YOUR TYPICAL DAY. A day of solving 1,000 creative puzzles and putting out fires, good food, e-mails, a swim or dance class if the planets align, dig my way out of e-mail quicksand, in bed by 10 and up by 5.

WHAT ADJECTIVES DESCRIBE YOU? Loyal, intuitive, empathetic.

YOUR FAVORITE DRINK? Lemon verbena tea from my garden.

IF YOU WERE A COLOR, WHAT WOULD YOU BE? Somewhere between silver and blue.

WHAT ARE YOUR BIGGEST PET PEEVES? Clutter, the word "no," Styrofoam packing noodles!

IN YOUR NEXT LIFE, WHO WOULD YOU LIKE TO BE? I would like to look like Elizabeth Taylor, sing like Beyoncé, write like Annie Lamott, cook like Thomas Keller, help the world like Bono, dance like Janet Jackson, make people laugh like Billy Crystal . . . I could work with that.

YOUR CHILDHOOD OBSESSIONS? Tap dancing, my Suzy bake oven, and holding my breath underwater for as long as humanly possible.

WHAT ARE YOUR GUILTY PLEASURES? Watching *The Voice* and *Shark Tank;* late-night shopping on eBay for vintage cars.

WHAT'S THE MOST INTERESTING THING YOU HAVE EVER FOUND? A Georgian diamond mourning ring and an antique silver Italian serving cart.

Every time I try to buy something new, *I feel like I like what I have better.* Which is kind of a nice feeling.

I collect *interesting textiles* and Chinese export silver boats, decanters with *silver stoppers,* architectural and *design books.*

IF MONEY WERE NO OBJECT, WHAT ITEM WOULD YOU SPLURGE ON? A palazzo on Lake Como; taking five years off to travel around the world with my family.

WHO DO YOU LIVE WITH? My husband, my two gorgeous tennis-playing sons, 4 turtles, 12 koi fish, and a real pain in the ass of a raccoon who is wreaking havoc in the yard!

WHAT DO YOU LIKE ABOUT YOUR HOME? The tall ceilings, the gardens, the pool house, my black and dove gray tennis court.

HOW OFTEN DOES YOUR HOME CHANGE? I used to hear my kids hit the floor because I had moved a chair, but not that much lately.

THE MOST IMPORTANT
element of a house is the
KITCHEN DESIGN.

INSPIRED BY . . .

» Forties chic meets today's living

» Dark paints and lacquer

» Different variations of grays and silver

» Country and urban combined

» Ceiling heights

» West Coast grand

» Combines comfort with style

» Updates tradition

» Melding of genders

» Simplistic elegance

» Accents of white for a pop instead of color

ACKNOWLEDGMENTS

Thank you to wonderful friends for being part of this book: Gina, Jamie, Barry, Michael, Donna, Baby, Carina, Ray, Annabel, Miv, Fiona, Martyn, Christopher, Ursula, Adam, Gaby, and Windsor. Everyone has been so generous with their time, their friendship, and their homes. There is not a house here that I wouldn't want to live in.

Thanks to:

The photographers, Tim Beddow in particularly, Edward Addeo, Erik Kvalsvik, Ingrid Rasmussen, Jonathan Beckerman, Lyn McCarthy, Paulo & Gianni of Studio Immagine, Tim Street-Porter, and Victoria Pearson. Thanks to Towner Jones for the back cover art.

Matt and Josh at Period Media, who help to get the word out.

My team—Alex Parish, Jennifer Barry, and Lucilla Smith for lending such excellent support.

The Gibbs Smith team, with special thanks to Gibbs, who was enthusiastic about this book from the beginning; Madge Baird, and Melissa Dymock. This is the fifth we've done and I'm sure that working with me is like having triplets without an anesthetic—but it's my nighttime job!

Doug Turshen for the cover design.

Mel Bordeaux for being there to help Mrs. Malaprop.

And everyone else who was part of this project. You know who you are.

I'm really so proud of this book. All the interiors are extraordinary and a tribute to those who live in them.

Thank you, all.

18 17 16 15 14   5 4 3 2 1

End sheets are "Sidone," by Kathryn M. Ireland
Back cover illustration by Tonwen Jones

Published by
Gibbs Smith
P.O. Box 667
Layton, Utah 84041

1.800.835.4993 orders
www.gibbs-smith.com

Cover designed by Doug Turshen
Interiors designed by Kurt Hauser and Melissa Dymock
Printed and bound in Hong Kong

Gibbs Smith books are printed on paper produced from sustainable PEFC-certified
forest/controlled wood source. Learn more at www.pefc.org.
Printed and bound in Hong Kong

Library of Congress Control Number: 2014937862
ISBN: 978-1-4236-2189-8